Weather Contents

The Weather Around You

Step outside. Weather is all around. It is wind in your hair, sun on your skin, rain in your soggy shoes.

Lots of things you do depend on the weather. Should you ride your bike or curl up on the sofa and read? Should you wear shorts or long pants? Weather also affects how you feel. A rainy day might make you quiet and thoughtful. A sunny day might make you happy and excited.

WEATHER WRITE

Turn to the weather log on pages 30 and 31. As you use this book, record your daily weather observations on the log. To begin, write the name of the month at the top of the log. A sample entry is filled in for you.

What's the Weather Like?

Look at the pictures of different kinds of weather. Write words to describe each picture. Choose words from the box or think of other words.

hot	sunny	rainy
cool	damp	calm
freezing	breezy	drizzly
wet	dry	soggy
windy	still	humid
		chilly

_____

_____

_____

_____

_____

_____

_____

_____

_____

What Makes Weather?

Heat from the sun, or temperature, and the push of the air on the earth, or **air pressure**, make weather happen. Weather also happens because of **wind** and wetness in the air, or **moisture**.

Temperature

A **thermometer** measures temperature. The warmer the weather, the higher the liquid in a thermometer rises. Temperature is measured in degrees. These thermometers go up and down by two-degree steps from 0°.

WEATHER WRITE

Read the temperature on a thermometer hanging in a shady place. Record the temperature on the weather log. Add to the log every day at about the same time.

This thermometer says 32°, the temperature at which water freezes.

This thermometer says 76°.

This thermometer says 56°.

What's the Temperature?

Read the thermometers. Write each temperature in the box. Then draw a line from each child to the temperature for which he or she is dressed.

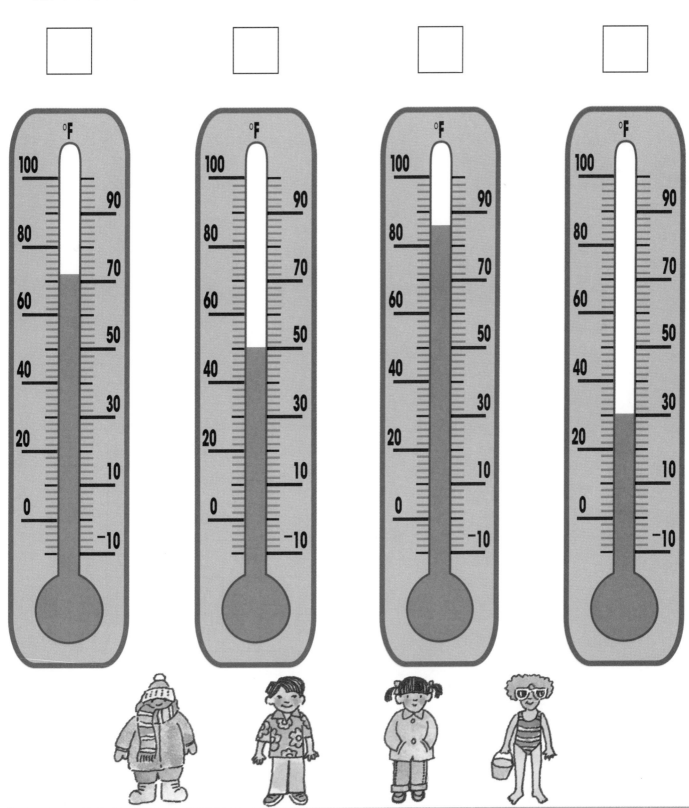

Wind

Wind is moving air. Some days are so still it seems that no air is moving at all. Don't be fooled, though. Air is always there, even when you don't notice it.

What makes wind? When air is warmed by the sun, it rises. Cold air rushes in to take its place. When that air is warmed by the sun, it rises, too. This happens over and over. We feel this movement of the air as wind.

Weather Report

Winds are described by the direction from which they blow. Southerly winds blow from the south. From which direction do northerly winds blow?

_____

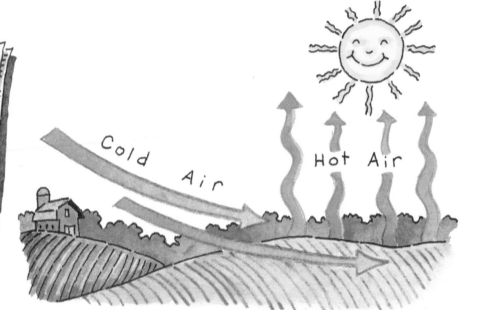

Cold Air

Hot Air

Airy Word Puzzle

Read the words in the box. They are some of the many words people use as they talk about moving air. How many of the words can you circle in the puzzle?

blast	draft
blow	gale
breeze	gust
current	wind

B	R	E	E	Z	E	W	B	A
H	L	F	S	T	E	I	L	X
D	C	U	R	R	E	N	T	B
F	N	S	D	L	N	D	E	L
O	T	N	R	X	T	P	E	O
I	S	L	A	B	R	O	D	W
V	S	T	F	G	A	L	E	E
G	U	S	T	T	E	R	G	S
U	B	L	A	S	T	H	L	P

Moisture

Water is what makes Earth different from other planets. Water makes life possible. It also helps make Earth's weather.

When water in oceans, lakes, and rivers is heated by the sun, some of it **evaporates**, or turns into an invisible gas called water vapor.

The Case of the Missing Water

Try this experiment with evaporation.

You need
- 2 clear measuring cups that are the same size

1 Fill both measuring cups about half full of water.

2 Place one uncovered measuring cup in a sunny indoor spot and the other cup in a shady indoor spot. From which measuring cup do you think the water will evaporate quicker?

_____

3 After a few days, check the cups. Has the water level changed? In what way? If not, wait a few more days. On the chart record the amount of water in each cup.

	Water in sun	Water in shade
Day 3		
Day 5		
Day 7		

From which cup did the water evaporate quicker? _____

Why? _____

Water vapor rises and cools. Cool air can't hold as much water vapor as warm air can, so some of the vapor turns into tiny drops of water. This is called condensation.

Dew and frost are two kinds of condensation. After a warm, dry day, water from air near the ground condenses as it cools. Drops of water called dew form. You can see dew on grass, spider webs, and everything else close to the ground. In cold weather, when the temperature goes below freezing, or 32°, dew changes to frost.

WORD WATCH

Precipitation is water in the form of rain, sleet, snow, or hail. Rain happens when the air is above freezing, or warmer than 32°. Sleet, snow, and hail happen when the air is below freezing.

Condensation on a Can

You need
• a can of soda or water

Put the can in the refrigerator. Leave it overnight. Next morning, take out the can and wait a minute or two. What do you see? Those drops are condensation. The can has cooled the air right next to it. You know that cold air can't hold as much water as warm air can, so the extra drops of water condense on the can.

Air Pressure

The weight of air pushing on the earth is called **air pressure**. Air pressure is another force that affects weather.

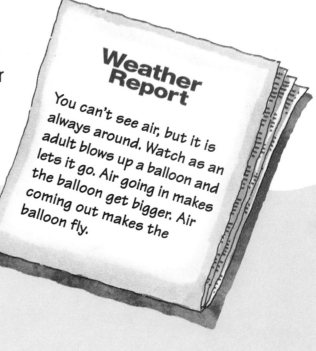

Weather Report

You can't see air, but it is always around. Watch as an adult blows up a balloon and lets it go. Air going in makes the balloon get bigger. Air coming out makes the balloon fly.

Air Pushes

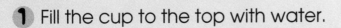
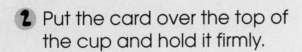

You need
- water
- plastic or foam cup
- postcard or index card

1 Fill the cup to the top with water.

2 Put the card over the top of the cup and hold it firmly.

What happens?

3 Still holding the card, turn the cup upside down. Let go of the card. (Do this over a sink.)

_____

_____

The card stays under the cup because of air pressure. The air under the card pushes up so strongly it keeps the card in place, even though the water in the cup is pushing down.

What Makes Weather? Puzzle

Write words from the box to complete the sentences.
Then fill in the puzzle.

ACROSS

1 What we wear depends on the _____.

6 Rain, snow, and hail are kinds of _____.

7 Drops of water on a cold can are _____.

wind
water
air pressure
precipitation
condensation
weather
Evaporation

DOWN

2 The push of air on the earth is _____.

3 _____ is what happens when water turns to water vapor.

4 Cold air can't hold as much _____ as warm air can.

5 Moving air is _____.

The Water Cycle

Tiny drops of water gather together and make clouds. When clouds have more water than the air can hold up, the water falls to Earth as rain or snow.

Water Travels

The water on Earth travels on an endless **cycle**, or journey. There are three steps to the water cycle: evaporation, condensation, and precipitation. Write the steps where they belong in the picture.

Water vapor makes a cloud.

Rain and snow fall from clouds.

Heat from the sun changes water into water vapor.

WORD WATCH

Meteorology is the science of weather. Weather scientists are called **meteorologists**.

Clouds

You've learned that clouds form when moist air rises and cools. Cool air can't hold as much water vapor as warm air. The water vapor starts to change into tiny drops of water or ice crystals that form clouds.

Cloud Shapes

Maybe you've looked at clouds in the sky and seen a dog, a tree, or some other shape. Look at the clouds in the picture. Circle the hidden shapes. How many can you find?

Different kinds of clouds bring different weather.

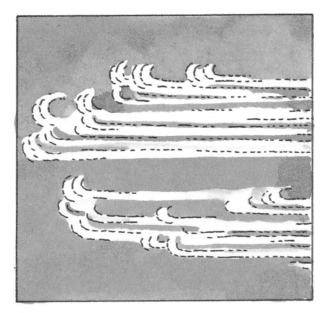

Cirrus clouds are thin wispy streaks high in the sky. They are so high that the water inside them is ice.

Cumulonimbus clouds are large gray thunderclouds. Thunderstorms and even tornadoes may come from these clouds.

Cumulus clouds look like big puffy heaps or piles. They may start near the ground and rise into the sky like big towers.

Stratus clouds are thick, even layers low in the sky. They often make drizzling rain or snow.

Watch out! Right now, I'm feeling like a cumulonimbus!

Clouds are always changing. That's because the moisture at the edges of the clouds evaporates. Another reason clouds change is that the wind blows them.

WEATHER WRITE

Check the sky each day.
Do you see any clouds?
What kind are they?
Write the cloud names.

Cloudy Riddles

Write cloud names to answer the riddles.

cumulonimbus
cirrus
stratus
cumulus

1 I look like a big, fluffy cotton puff. Who am I? _____

2 I'm dark and I can be noisy. People go inside when they see me. Who am I? _____

3 I'm light and feathery. Who am I? _____

4 I like to spread out. When I'm in a gray mood, I drizzle. Who am I?

_____

Fantastic Cloud Maker

With a little help you can make your own cloud.

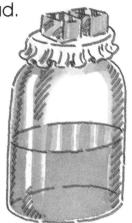

You need
- a clear glass jar
- plastic wrap
- ice
- hot tap water

1 Ask an adult to fill a jar with hot tap water and then pour out half the water.

2 Cover the jar with plastic wrap. Be careful not to burn your hands on the jar.

3 Place several ice cubes on top of the plastic wrap.

What do you see?

_____

_____

_____

Why did it happen? (Turn back to page 11 for help.)

_____

_____

_____

WORD WATCH

Fog is a stratus cloud at ground level. Like a cloud, fog contains millions of tiny water drops. Fog forms when water vapor condenses near the ground. **Mist** is like fog, except much thinner. **Smog** happens when smoke and other kinds of dirt mix with fog.

Weather Events

Rain and Rainbows

When the water inside a cloud is too heavy for the air to hold up, rain falls.

Make a Rain Gauge

You need

- a measuring cup

2 CUPS

1½

1 CUP

½

Make a rain gauge to measure the amount of rain that falls where you live. Here's how.
   Put a measuring cup outside where it will collect rainwater. Each week record the amount of rain in the measuring cup in your weather log. Compare rainfall from week to week.

Rainbows are arcs of colors seen in the sky opposite the sun. They are caused by sunlight shining through small drops of water. Rainbows are made of red, orange, yellow, green, blue, indigo, and violet light. The colors in a rainbow are always in the same order.

Weather Report

Here's a way to remember the colors in a rainbow in the right order. Think of the name Roy G. Biv. Each letter stands for a color in the rainbow, starting with red at the top and ending with violet.

Your Own Rainbow

On a sunny day, you can make your own rainbow.

You need
- a large glass of water
- a piece of white paper
- crayons or colored markers

Place the glass of water on a sunny indoor windowsill. Put a piece of white paper on a table beside the windowsill. Slide the paper around on the table until colors appear on the paper. You've made a rainbow!
Color the rainbow. Make sure the colors are in the right order.

Thunderstorms

Thunderstorms are caused by electricity that builds up in clouds. When the electricity is strong enough, a spark leaps from one cloud to another or to the ground. That spark is **lightning**. As lightning travels, the heated air around it expands so quickly that it explodes, making the loud noise we call **thunder**. Although thunder and lightning happen at the same time, you see lightning before you hear thunder because light travels much faster than sound.

How did the lightning leave the party?

In a flash.

You're Electric!

You need

• a balloon

Electricity is around you all the time. There is even some in your body.

Try this simple experiment. Rub an air-filled balloon on your clothes. Press the balloon against a smooth wall. Static electricity will make the balloon cling. Rub the balloon again and see what happens when you touch it to your hair.

Snowstorms

Snow forms when ice crystals in a cloud bump into each other and stick together. If the air temperature below the cloud is cold enough, snow falls.

Weather Report

All snowflakes have six sides. Some snowflakes are made of as many as 100 ice crystals. No two snowflakes are alike.

Flake Detective

You need
- black construction paper
- magnifying glass

On the next snowy day, put a piece of black construction paper in the refrigerator for a few minutes. Then take the paper outside and place it on the ground. Look through a magnifying glass at some of the snowflakes that land on the paper. (Don't breathe on the flakes! You'll melt them.) Draw what you see.

Blizzards are very bad snowstorms. They bring strong winds and lots of snow, either falling from the sky or being blown about by the gusty wind. Blizzards are dangerous because it's hard to see and temperatures are very low. Some blizzards are so severe that people in the country have gotten lost going from their house to their mailbox!

Homeward Bound

Find your way home through the snowstorm. Watch out for snowbanks!

Tornadoes

Tornadoes are big whirlwinds of air that can swirl faster than 200 miles an hour. They may happen when a mass of cool, dry air runs into a mass of warm, damp air. The warm air rises quickly, thunderclouds form, and a twisting funnel of air begins to spin downward.

When tornadoes move on land, they can destroy everything they touch. Like huge vacuum cleaners, they suck up things in their paths.

Twister Fixer

A tornado has picked up things and dropped them in the wrong places. Circle the misplaced objects.

Tornadoes may not move at all, or they may travel as fast as 70 mph. They happen most often in the midwest and some southern parts of the United States in spring and early summer.

What are sleeping twisters?

Tornadoze.

Tornado Nicknames

The words in the box are some of the many names for tornadoes. How many can you find in the puzzle? Circle them.

cyclone	**spinner**
twister	**vortex**
funnel	**churn**
whirlwind	

W	H	I	R	L	W	I	N	D
H	L	F	X	P	I	N	L	X
D	C	Y	C	L	O	N	E	T
F	U	N	N	E	L	D	V	W
O	T	N	R	C	T	P	O	I
F	N	S	D	H	J	G	R	S
V	S	T	B	U	N	L	T	T
G	P	S	T	R	K	R	E	E
S	P	I	N	N	E	R	X	R

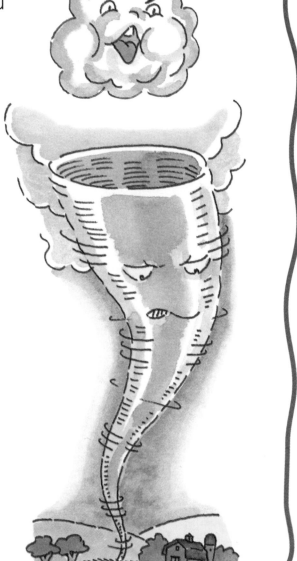

Hurricanes

Like tornadoes, **hurricanes** are powerful, whirling storms. Hurricanes are much larger than tornadoes, though. Hurricanes form over warm oceans and can travel hundreds of miles.

As the summer sun heats the sea, warm water vapor rises into the air and forms large thunderclouds. If there is wind, masses of clouds may begin to whirl strongly. As hurricanes move over the ocean, they create huge waves that can crash on shore. Hurricanes may move over land, bringing high winds and heavy rains.

Weather Report

To keep track of the hurricanes that happen each year, meteorologists name them. The first hurricane of the new year is given a name starting with the letter A. The next hurricane is given a name starting with B, and so on.

Get to the Eye!

The eye of a hurricane is the calm part at the center. Find your way through the hurricane to its eye.

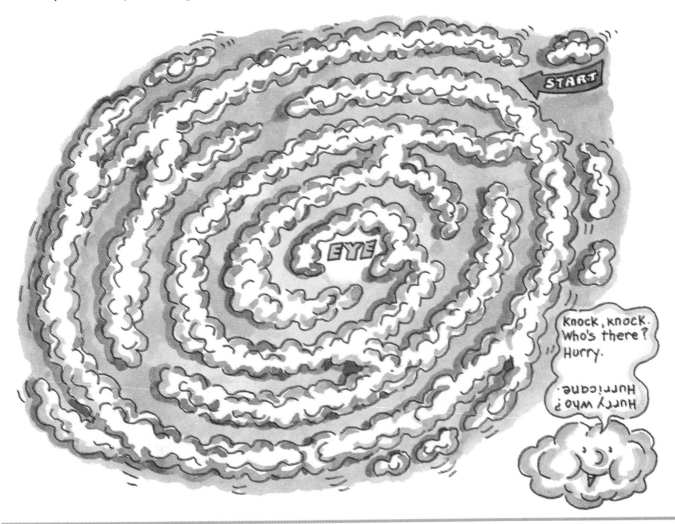

What Am I?

Write a word from the box after each clue.

WEATHER WRITE

During hurricane season, watch the news for reports of hurricanes. Keep track of each hurricane's name and where the hurricane starts and ends.

tornado
thunderstorm
rainbow
hurricane
snowstorm

1 My favorite dance is the twist. What am I?

_____

2 I turn everything white. What am I?

_____

3 I'm bigger and badder than a tornado. What am I?

_____

4 When I rain, I pour, and pour some more. What am I?

_____

5 I'm one of the prettiest things that comes with rain. What am I?

_____

Watching the Weather

Checking the weather is one of the first things many people do each day, especially people who work outdoors.

Outdoors in All Kinds of Weather

This puzzle includes some of the outdoor activities affected by the weather. Write words from the box to complete the puzzle.

- mail carrier
- farmer
- skier
- crossing guard
- golfer
- gardener
- climber
- fisherman
- pilot
- driver

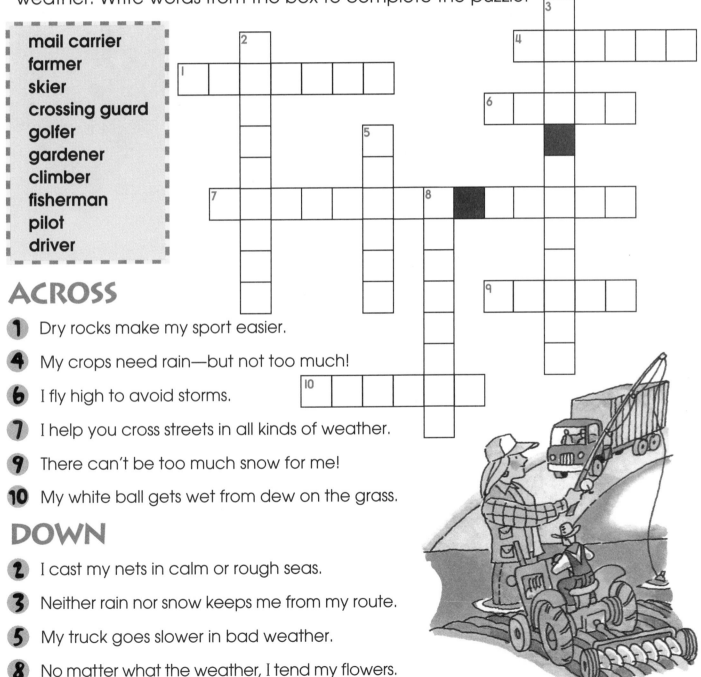

ACROSS

1. Dry rocks make my sport easier.
4. My crops need rain—but not too much!
6. I fly high to avoid storms.
7. I help you cross streets in all kinds of weather.
9. There can't be too much snow for me!
10. My white ball gets wet from dew on the grass.

DOWN

2. I cast my nets in calm or rough seas.
3. Neither rain nor snow keeps me from my route.
5. My truck goes slower in bad weather.
8. No matter what the weather, I tend my flowers.

People have many beliefs about weather. Some of them are true, but others are superstitions.

Fact: People use pine cones as weather gauges. In dry weather, pine cones dry out and open. When rain is coming, pine cones absorb water in the air and close up.

Fact: Have you noticed that crickets chirp louder in hot weather? When it's warm, adding 37 to the number of chirps you hear in 15 seconds will about equal the temperature.

Superstition: Custom says that if a groundhog comes out of its hole and sees its shadow on February 2, winter weather will last for six more weeks.

Superstition: Some people believe that woolly bear caterpillars' stripes can predict whether a winter will be mild or severe. They think that if the caterpillars' brown stripes are wider than the black stripes, winter will be mild. If the black stripes are wider, winter will be severe. Scientists say that the size of its stripes has to do with the age of a woolly bear caterpillar.

Superstitions: Many people believe that birds go back to their nests before storms. Some people think the early or late migration of birds can predict whether winter will come early or late.

Fact or Superstition? Red sky at night, sailors' delight. Red sky at morning, sailors take warning.

This old saying means that a red sunset will be followed by good weather, and a red sunrise will bring storms. Watch the sunsets where you live. What do you notice?

_____

_____

_____

Find the Secret Words

Answer the questions. Then fill in the numbered boxes.

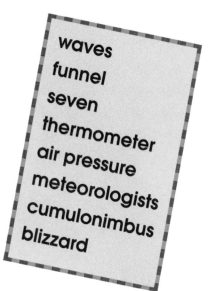

waves
funnel
seven
thermometer
air pressure
meteorologists
cumulonimbus
blizzard

1 Four forces that make weather are heat, moisture,

$\underline{}\ \underline{}\ \underline{}$ $\underline{}\ \underline{}\ \underline{}\ \underline{}\ \underline{}\ \underline{}\ \underline{}\ \underline{}$, and wind.
6 10

2 We use a $\underline{}\ \underline{}\ \underline{}\ \underline{}\ \underline{}\ \underline{}\ \underline{}\ \underline{}\ \underline{}\ \underline{}$ to measure temperature.
9 2 7

3 Thunderstorms come from $\underline{}\ \underline{}\ \underline{}\ \underline{}\ \underline{}\ \underline{}\ \underline{}\ \underline{}\ \underline{}\ \underline{}\ \underline{}$ clouds.
3

4 Rainbows have $\underline{}\ \underline{}\ \underline{}\ \underline{}\ \underline{}$ colors.
5

5 A very bad snowstorm is called a $\underline{}\ \underline{}\ \underline{}\ \underline{}\ \underline{}\ \underline{}\ \underline{}\ \underline{}$.
1

6 A tornado is a big whirlwind of air shaped like a $\underline{}\ \underline{}\ \underline{}\ \underline{}\ \underline{}\ \underline{}$.
11

7 Hurricanes make $\underline{}\ \underline{}\ \underline{}\ \underline{}\ \underline{}$ as they race over the ocean.
8 12

8 Scientists called $\underline{}\ \underline{}\ \underline{}\ \underline{}\ \underline{}\ \underline{}\ \underline{}\ \underline{}\ \underline{}\ \underline{}\ \underline{}\ \underline{}\ \underline{}$ study weather.
4

Write the letters with numbers under them in the boxes
to describe yourself.

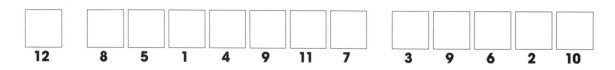

12 8 5 1 4 9 11 7 3 9 6 2 10

More About Weather

Information Books

Flash, Crash, Rumble and Roll by Franklin M. Branley
Flood by Julia Waterlow
Hurricanes and Tornadoes by Norman S. Barrett
Storm by Jenny Wood
The Super Science Book of Weather by Key Davies
   and Wendy Oldfield
Weather by Brian Cosgrove
Weather Forecasting by Gail Gibbons
Weather Words by Gail Gibbons

CD-ROM

Weather Trackers by Aaron Gregory

Videocassette

The Unchained Goddess by Frank Capra

Storybooks and Poetry

It Looked Like Spilt Milk by Charles G. Shaw
Rainy Day Rhymes by Gail Radley
The Snowy Day by Ezra Jack Keats
Thunder Cake by Patricia Polacco

Weather Log

MONTH

Day	Temperature	Rainfall	Type of Weather
	89°	1/2"	
1			
2			
3			
4			
5			
6			
7			
8			
9			
10			
11			
12			
13			
14			
15			
16			

Types of Weather

rainy

snowy

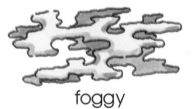

foggy

cloudy

partly cloudy

sunny

Day	Temperature	Rainfall	Type of Weather
17			
18			
19			
20			
21			
22			
23			
24			
25			
26			
27			
28			
29			
30			
31			

Look at the information on the weather log.

Has the weather gotten warmer or cooler during the month?

_____

How much rain fell?

_____

Which type of weather happened most often?

_____

Answers

Page 3
Possible answers include hot, sunny and dry for the first picture; windy, cool, breezy, and dry for the second picture; and wet, drizzly, and soggy for the third picture.

Page 5
72°, 50°, 86°, 30°

Page 6

B	R	E	E	Z	E	W	B	A
H	L	F	S	T	E	I	L	X
D	C	U	R	R	E	N	T	B
F	N	S	D	L	N	D	E	L
O	T	N	R	X	T	P	E	O
I	S	L	A	B	R	O	D	W
V	S	T	F	G	A	L	E	E
G	U	S	T	T	E	R	G	S
U	B	L	A	S	T	H	L	P

Page 10

1. WEATHER
2. EVAPORATION
3. AIR PRESSURE
4. WATER
5. WIND
6. PRECIPITATION
7. CONDENSATION

Page 11
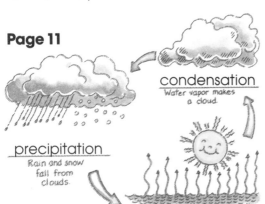

condensation
Water vapor makes a cloud.

precipitation
Rain and snow fall from clouds.

evaporation
Heat from the sun changes water into water vapor.

Page 12

Page 14
1. cumulus
2. cumulonimbus
3. cirrus
4. stratus

Page 17
The colors in the rainbow are always in the same order: red, orange, yellow, green, blue, indigo, and violet.

Page 20

Page 21

Page 22

W	H	I	R	L	W	I	N	D
H	L	F	X	P	I	N	L	X
D	C	Y	C	L	O	N	E	T
F	U	N	N	E	L	D	V	W
O	T	N	R	C	T	P	O	I
F	N	S	D	H	J	G	R	S
V	S	T	B	U	N	L	T	T
G	P	S	T	R	K	R	E	E
S	P	I	N	N	E	R	X	R

Page 23

Page 24
1. tornado
2. snowstorm
3. hurricane
4. thunderstorm
5. rainbow

Page 25

1. CLIMBER
2. FISHERMAN
3. FARMER
4. DRIVER
5. PILOT
6. CROSSING GUARD
7. GARDENER
8. CARRIER
9. SKIER
10. GOLFER

Page 28
1. air pressure
2. thermometer
3. cumulonimbus
4. seven
5. blizzard
6. funnel
7. waves
8. meteorologists

a weather champ

Seeds & Plants Contents

What Is a Seed?

Have you ever seen a seed? Maybe you took a bite of a juicy red apple and saw the small seeds inside. Perhaps you helped plant flower seeds or watched a squirrel gather acorns.

A seed is a package of plant life. Each seed has a little plant inside. Many seeds hold food, too.

Seeds are made by the male and female parts of flowers. Most seeds live inside fruit until they are ready to begin to grow into plants.

Plant Some Seeds

Plant sunflower seeds in the garden. Follow the arrow to plant the seeds.

Look Inside a Seed

You wear a coat to protect you from the cold. Seeds from flowering plants have **seed coats** to protect them. Inside the seed are one or two **food storage** parts. Next to the food storage parts is a baby plant, the **embryo** (**em**-bree-oh). The embryo has tiny leaves, a stem, and roots.

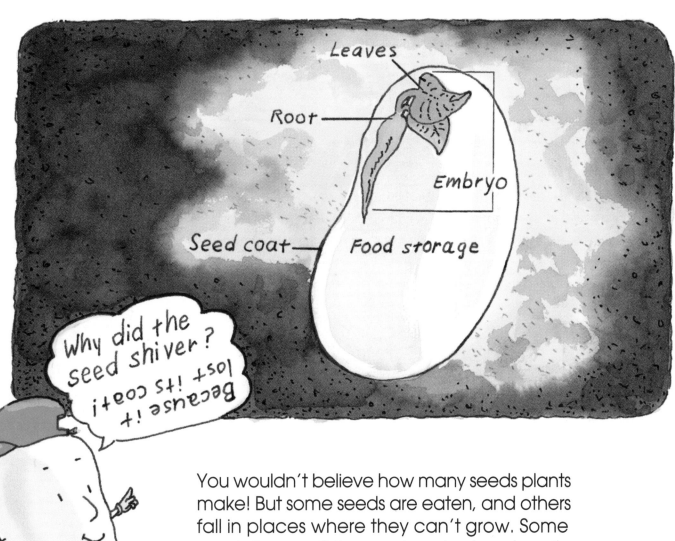

Leaves

Root

Embryo

Seed coat

Food storage

Why did the seed shiver?

Because it lost its coat!

You wouldn't believe how many seeds plants make! But some seeds are eaten, and others fall in places where they can't grow. Some seeds freeze. Others get soaked and spoil. A few seeds, though, end up in places where they get the right temperature and enough air, water, and light to begin to grow, or **germinate** (**jur**-muh-nate).

©1997 School Zone Publishing Company

Would you like to see the inside of a seed?
Let's look inside one kind of seed—a lima bean.

A Seed from the Outside In

YOU NEED

• dried lima bean
• cup of water
• hand lens

1 Fill a cup with water.

2 Put the lima bean in the water.

3 Leave the bean overnight.

4 Take the lima bean out of the water and look at it. Use a hand lens, if you have one.

What happened to the outside of the seed? Try to peel off the seed covering. Split the seed into halves. Look for the parts shown in the picture on page 35. Draw the lima bean. Write the names of the parts of the seed where they belong.

Food storage
Seed coat
Leaves
Roots
Embryo

Seedy Word Puzzle

Write a word from the pot after each clue.
Then circle the words in the puzzle.

stem **water** **plants** **seeds** **embryo**

1. Seeds come from _____ .

2. a baby plant inside a seed _____

3. one of the tiny parts inside the embryo _____

4. Seeds need _____ to grow.

5. Not all _____ grow into plants.

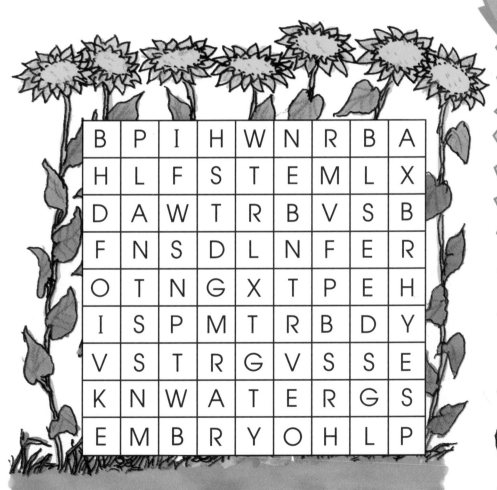

B	P	I	H	W	N	R	B	A
H	L	F	S	T	E	M	L	X
D	A	W	T	R	B	V	S	B
F	N	S	D	L	N	F	E	R
O	T	N	G	X	T	P	E	H
I	S	P	M	T	R	B	D	Y
V	S	T	R	G	V	S	S	E
K	N	W	A	T	E	R	G	S
E	M	B	R	Y	O	H	L	P

Most plants grow from seeds. But some can grow from other plant parts. Onions make parts that turn into **bulbs** and new plants. The bulbs are the part we eat.

Potato plants grow from **tubers**, thick parts of the stem that grow underground. Tubers can grow into plants. Tubers are the part we eat.

Seeds Come in All Shapes and Sizes

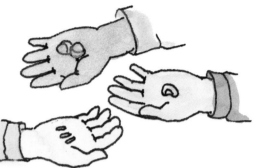

Just like people, seeds come in all shapes and sizes. Lima beans are fairly large seeds. Petunia seeds are so small you can hardly see them.

Many seeds have a cover, such as a fruit, a shell, or a pod. Can you think of any like this?

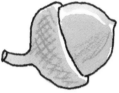

Acorn

Maple

Wild carrot

Lettuce

Wild rice

Poppy

Watermelon

An Ounce of Seeds

YOU NEED

- clear measuring cup
- lots of sunflower seeds

1 Have an adult help you fill the measuring cup to the one ounce mark with sunflower seeds. How many seeds do you think are in one ounce?

_____

2 Pour out the seeds and count them. How many sunflower seeds are in one ounce?

_____

How close was your estimate?

_____

Name That Seed

Look at the seeds. You might find them in
a yard, garden, or grocery store. Write the
name of each seed on the line under its picture.

watermelon
coconut
corn

_____ _____ _____

1. Will the **largest** seed grow into the largest plant?
Take a guess. Check **yes** or **no**.

yes   no

2. Will the **smallest** seed grow into the smallest plant?
Guess again. Check **yes** or **no**.

yes   no

The milkweed seed is
larger than the giant
sequoia (suh-**kwoi**-uh)
tree seed. But the
milkweed plant grows
to be only a few feet tall,
while the sequoia tree
can grow to be more
than 300 feet high.

Look at the seeds and the plants into which they grow. Did you identify each kind of seed correctly? If not, turn back to page 39 and write the correct names.

Compare the size of the seeds with the size of the plants. Small seeds can grow into large plants. Big seeds can become small plants. Seed size has nothing to do with the size of a plant.

Corn   **Coconut palm**   **Watermelon**

Roasted Pumpkin Seeds

YOU NEED
- pumpkin seeds
- cookie sheet
- vegetable oil
- salt

1. Have an adult turn the oven to 250°.
2. Wash and dry some pumpkin seeds.
3. Pour a light coat of vegetable oil on a cookie sheet.
4. Spread the pumpkin seeds evenly over the sheet. Put salt on them, if you like.
5. Bake the seeds for about 15 minutes. Have the adult stir the seeds so they don't burn and return them to the oven for about 15 minutes more. When they turn golden brown, the seeds are done.
6. Cool the seeds. Share them with a friend.

YOU NEED

- newspaper
- seeds of different sizes and shapes
- white glue
- cardboard or heavy paper

Make a Seed Picture

Put newspaper over your work area. Then set out your materials.

Cover the cardboard or heavy paper with glue. Arrange the seeds in a design you like. (Be sure to push the big seeds firmly into the glue.) Let your seed picture dry overnight.

It's in Code!

Fill in the missing code numbers. Then use the code to find the name of a large fruit that starts as a small seed. Write the name of the fruit on the line.

a = 5	b =	c = 15
d =	e = 25	f = 30
g =	h = 40	i =
j =	k =	l = 60
m = 65	n =	o =
p =	q = 85	r =
s = 95	t = 100	u = 105
v =	w = 115	x =
y = 125	z = 130	

80 105 65 80 55 45 70

____ ____ ____ ____ ____ ____ ____

The largest seeds in the world come from the coco-de-mer tree. (**Coco-de-mer** means "nut of the sea.") One nut can weigh more than 50 pounds. That may be almost as much as you weigh.

How Seeds Travel

Imagine you live in a house with ten brothers and sisters. The family grows up, but no one moves out. You all get married and have children, still living in the same house together. Everyone is crowded!

Plants are like people that way. If they dropped their seeds right beside them, the seeds would be crowded too close together. Seeds have several ways to keep this from happening. One way is for animals to carry seeds to places where the seeds may have more room to grow.

Seeds Hitch a Ride

Spanish needles

Burdock

The seeds from these plants move from place to place by sticking to animal fur.

The seeds have ___ ___ ___ ___ ___ or
       3 5 5 4 7

___ ___ ___ ___ ___ to help them cling.
2 1 6 2 7

Use the code to figure out the missing words.

Code

1 = a
2 = b
3 = h
4 = k
5 = o
6 = r
7 = s

Seed Safari

YOU NEED
- old white socks
- big piece of white paper

Put the socks on over your shoes. Take a walk with an adult through a weedy vacant lot, a field, or a park.

When you get home, take off the socks carefully. Shake them out over the paper. What do you see? Have any seeds stuck to the socks?

After they eat berries and other fruit, birds drop some of the seeds as they fly. This is another way that seeds are moved from place to place. Some seeds birds scatter are thistle seeds, apple seeds, and mistletoe seeds.

Drop a Berry in the Meadow

Help the cardinal find its way to the meadow, where it will drop the berry and scatter the seeds inside.

MEADOW

Do you ever forget things? Squirrels do! Sometimes squirrels bury acorns and forget where they are. Some of the acorns grow into oak trees. Being buried by animals is another way seeds move.

Find the Acorns

Help the squirrel find the acorns it buried. Circle ten hidden acorns.

The wind moves some seeds from place to place. Have you ever blown on the soft, white seeds of a dandelion? Did the seeds fly through the air? Your breath was like a puff of wind.

Dandelion seeds aren't the only kind moved by wind

pine

cottonwood

Maple

Milkweed

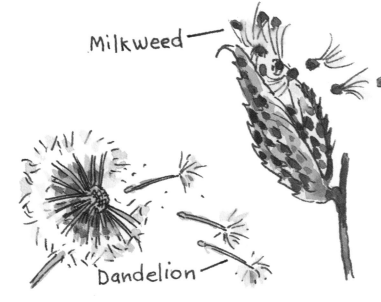

Dandelion

Have you ever seen a tumbleweed on the western plains? Tumbleweeds roll into a ball when their seeds are ripe, and their roots dry up. When a wind comes, the whole plant blows away, scattering seeds as it goes.

WRITE NOW!
Splash! You're a coconut that has just fallen from a palm tree into the ocean. Take out a sheet of paper, and write what happens to you.

Some plants drop their seeds near water. The water carries the seeds—sometimes to places where they can grow. Pussy willow seeds can be moved by water. Coconut seeds can fall into the ocean and grow into new plants if they reach land again.

What Do Seeds Need to Grow?

Some seeds can wait a long time for everything to be just right so they can grow. If you look at a seed while it is waiting, you might see its wrinkled coat. The seed is not dead. It is just resting.

People need food to live and grow. Seeds do, too. Seeds need air, plenty of water, and the right temperature to germinate. Some seeds also need light.

Sprout a Seed

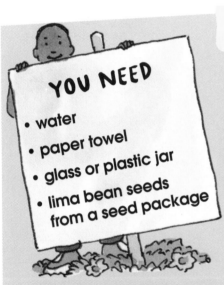

YOU NEED

- water
- paper towel
- glass or plastic jar
- lima bean seeds from a seed package

1 Wrap wet paper towels around the inside of a jar.

2 Have an adult help you fill the jar about one-fourth full with water.

3 Put a few lima beans between the inside of the jar and the paper towels.

4 Leave the jar on a windowsill in your house for about a week. Check each day to make sure the paper towels stay wet.

Your lima beans have germinated! They swelled up with water and broke through the seed coat. Lima beans are growing. The part growing up is the shoot. The part growing down is the root. Draw one of the seeds. Write **shoot** and **root** next to those parts.

WRITE NOW!
You find an odd-looking seed and plant it. Your seed grows into _____. Take out a sheet of paper. Write an ending to the story.

Some seeds are so small it's hard to see them. Here's a way to watch for shoots from seeds you can't see.

YOU NEED
- empty milk carton
- soil from a yard or garden
- water

1 Have an adult cut the milk carton in half.
2 Fill the bottom half with soil.
3 Move the carton to a shady place inside the house.
4 Water the soil daily to keep it moist.
5 Put a check mark on the chart by the day you see the first shoots.

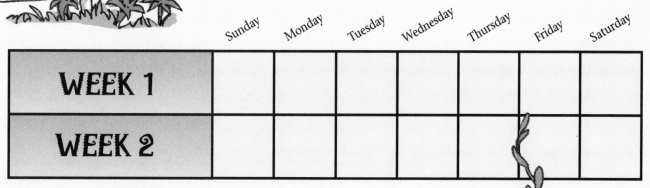

	Sunday	Monday	Tuesday	Wednesday	Thursday	Friday	Saturday
WEEK 1							
WEEK 2							

Look at the chart. How many days did it take for the first seed to sprout?

_____

Seed Riddles

coat   leaves   germinate   roots   stem

Solve the riddles with words from the pot.

1. A seed doesn't have a hat, but it does have a _____ .

2. A seed has no flowers, but it does have a _____ ,

_____ , and _____ .

3. A seed doesn't have germs, but it does _____ .

From Seed to Plant

This is how a new plant grows from a seed.

- The seed swells with water and bursts through its seed coat, or germinates.

- The roots grow down into the soil.

- The shoot grows up toward the sunlight. Leaves grow from the shoot.

- The plant gets bigger each day.

- Buds appear on the plant.

- Blossoms appear on the plant.

Sunflowers need so much sunlight they turn their heads during the day to face the sun.

The plant is fully grown. It will have fruit with seeds inside. After a while the fruit will ripen and the seeds will spill out. Some of the seeds will germinate and more plants will grow.

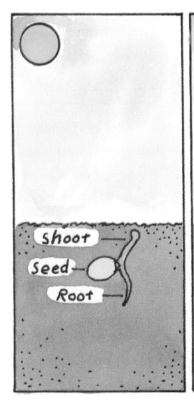

Write the Parts

Write the names of the plant parts on the lines.

_____

_____

_____

_____

The study of plants is called **botany**. A scientist who studies plants is a **botanist**.

What's That Sound?

YOU NEED
- cup of popcorn
- water
- baking pan

Fill a cup nearly to the top with popcorn kernels. Add water to fill the cup completely. Then put the cup in a baking pan. Wait five or six hours. You'll hear some surprising sounds! What might the sounds be?

A Plant Grows Up

What's wrong with these pictures? A flowering plant is growing, but the order is all mixed up. Number the pictures from 1 to 6 in the correct order.

_____

_____

_____

_____

_____

_____

Plant Words

Answer the questions with words from the pot. Then look for the answers in the puzzle. Circle the words.

buds
shoot   soil
energy
stem   root

1. What is the earth in which seeds grow called?

_____

2. What is the part of a seed that grows up?

_____

3. What is the part of a seed that grows down?

_____

4. What do plants get from the sun that helps them grow?

_____

5. What appears before blossoms on a plant?

_____

6. What does water travel through after it comes up a plant's roots?

_____

What's the saddest seed?

A weeping willow!

E	N	E	R	G	Y	R	B	A
H	L	F	S	O	I	L	H	X
D	K	W	T	X	B	Z	R	B
F	N	S	D	C	N	F	O	R
O	S	T	C	B	T	P	O	H
I	T	Z	M	U	R	V	T	Y
V	E	T	R	D	V	S	N	E
K	M	W	F	S	H	O	O	T
U	P	O	T	B	I	H	L	P

Plants Are Partners

Plants take in air through tiny holes in their leaves. Plants take in water through the roots, up the stem, and into the leaves. Sunlight makes the air and water join to create the energy plants need to grow. New plants turn their leaves toward the light. They want to get as much energy as they can!

Animals and plants are partners. Here's how. Take a big breath of air. You just took in a gas called **oxygen**. Some of that oxygen comes from plants. Now breathe out. You just put a gas called **carbon dioxide** into the air. Plants use the carbon dioxide to make their food.

Stem

Root

See Water Travel

YOU NEED
- food coloring
- stalk of celery with leaves
- glass of water

1 Ask an adult to put a few drops of red or blue food coloring in a glass of water. Place a stalk of celery with leaves into the glass, leaf end up.

2 Wait a few hours. What happened to the celery? Ask the adult to slice the celery the short way. Look at the colored paths in the celery that carry water.

You know that plants grow by taking energy from the sun, carbon dioxide from the air, and water from the ground. They give us food to eat and oxygen to breathe. This partnership is called the cycle of nature. (A **cycle** is something that is repeated.)

The cycle starts with the sun's energy. It ends when plants and animals die and return to the ground. There they add minerals to the soil. Then plants take in the minerals with water from the soil. The cycle begins all over again.

Cycle of Nature

1. What do plants get from the air? _____

2. How does it get into the air? _____

3. What do animals get from the air? _____

4. How does it get into the air? _____

All Kinds of Plants Grow from Seeds

Some seeds grow into plants with flowers that make gardens beautiful and sweet smelling. Some seeds become trees and bushes that shade people and give wood. Some seeds grow into plants that give tasty fruits and vegetables.

What's Growing?

The seeds in these pots are growing into plants. But what kind of plants are they? Read the clues. Then write the name of each plant under its pot.

corn
lily
bean
tomato

The name of this plant rhymes with **potato**.

1. _____

The name of this plant rhymes with **mean**.

2. _____

The name of this plant rhymes with **horn**.

3. _____

The name of this plant rhymes with **silly**.

4. _____

How Fast Do Plants Grow?

Here's another way plants are like people. Some grow slowly; others grow quickly. This year you might have been like many trees, growing slowly and steadily. Or maybe you grew quickly, as a radish plant does.

How Much Did It Grow?

These four plants have been growing for three weeks. How much did they grow? Read the graph. Then answer the questions.

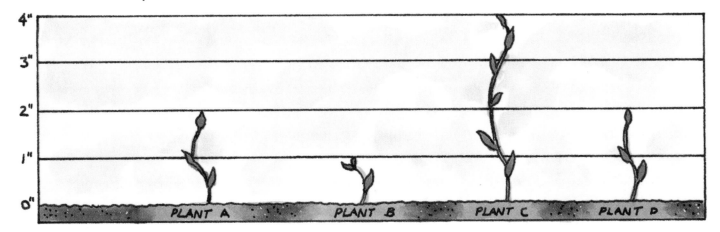

1. Which plant grew the most?

_____

2. How much taller is the biggest plant than the smallest one?

_____

3. Which two plants grew the same amount?

_____

_____

One kind of plant, bamboo, can grow as many as three feet in one day!

How Plants Protect Themselves

Some plants protect themselves from insects and other animals that would like to eat them. Spines, thorns, and prickles keep away large animals. Coatings of wax or stiff hairs on leaves keep away smaller ones. And what insect would want to eat leaves that taste terrible, such as those of citrus plants, or are poisonous, such as those of nightshade or foxglove?

Rose

Cactus

Poison Ivy

Another way that plants protect themselves is through **camouflage** (**kam**-uh-flazh), coverings or colors that make plants blend with their surroundings.

A Plant Fights Back

Think of a way a plant might protect itself. Draw your plant here.

Some plants don't have to worry about being eaten by animals. They eat animals instead. One of those plants, the Venus's-flytrap, has leaves that snap shut when an insect lands on them. The leaves open up again after the insect has been eaten.

Plants and Animals

Plants and animals help each other in different ways.

Helpers, Inc.

Read the clues. Write words from the pot that fit the shapes.

food
drop   bury
       hide
carry seeds

1. Many animals need plants for ☐☐☐☐ .

2. Many animals eat ☐☐☐☐ .

3. Animals use plants to ☐☐☐ .

4. Squirrels ☐☐☐☐ nuts.

5. Animals ☐☐☐☐☐ seeds on their fur.

6. Birds ☐☐☐☐ seeds as they fly.

Plant Parts We Love to Eat

People and animals eat the fruits of some plants, the seeds of some, and the leaves and roots of others.

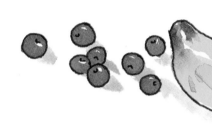

Do you recognize these plants? The one on the left is a sweet potato. What part do we eat? The one on the right is corn. What part of the corn plant do we eat?

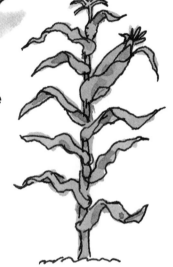

1. _____

2. _____

These are different kinds of lettuce. What part of the plant do we eat?

3. _____

People Need Plants

Plants give us food. List some fruits and vegetables and foods made from fruits and vegetables that we eat.

There are more than 350,000 different kinds of plants!

_____

_____

Plants are made into fiber for clothing. What other kinds of clothes could be made from fiber?

_____

_____

Trees are plants that give us wood for buildings and for fuel. Paper comes from trees, too. Can you think of anything else people use that comes from trees?

Many animals, including cows, pigs, and chickens, eat plants. Then cows give us milk, pigs provide meat, and chickens lay eggs. Write the name of another animal that eats plants.

Some plants make problems for people. Weeds can crowd out flowers in a garden or crops in a field. Some plants cause sneezes and itchy eyes. Others, such as poison ivy, bother the skin.

But plants help far more than they hurt. They keep the soil from blowing away. They slow down rushing water by holding some of it in their roots and stems. They are food for animals. The whole world needs plants. And most plants start with seeds.

WRITE NOW!
Imagine a world without plants. On a sheet of paper describe what that world would be like.

The Truth About Seeds and Plants

You know a lot about seeds and plants! Take this quiz. Write true if the sentence is true. Write **false** if the sentence is not true. If you don't remember, look on the page or pages listed after the sentence.

1. Most seeds live inside fruit until they are ready to begin to grow. (p. 34)_____

2. The embryo of a seed has tiny fruits inside. (p. 35)_____

3. All seeds germinate. (p. 35)_____

4. All seeds are the same shape and size. (p. 38)_____

5. One way seeds travel is by sticking to animal fur. (p. 42) _____

6. Shoots grow down into the soil, and roots grow up toward the sun. (p. 46) _____

7. Buds appear before blossoms on a plant. (p. 48) _____

8. Plants need energy to grow. (p. 52) _____

9. Plants have thorns to attract insects. (p. 56) _____

10. People need plants to live. (p. 59-61) _____

Answers

Page 34

Page 36
Labels should include
Seed coat, Food storage,
Leaves, Roots, Embryo

Page 37
1. plants
2. embryo
3. stem
4. water
5. seeds

B	P	I	H	W	N	R	B	A
H	L	F	S	T	E	M	L	X
D	A	W	T	R	B	V	S	B
F	N	S	D	L	N	F	E	R
O	T	N	G	X	T	P	E	H
I	S	P	M	T	R	B	D	Y
V	S	T	R	G	V	S	S	E
K	N	W	A	T	E	R	G	S
E	M	B	R	Y	O	H	L	P

Page 38
Answers
will vary.

Page 39
1. no
2. no

Page 41
pumpkin

Page 42
hooks, barbs

Page 43

Page 44

Page 46
Children's drawings should
include labels that identify the
part of the plant growing up as
the shoot and the part growing
down as the root.

Page 47
1. coat
2. stem, leaves,
   roots
3. germinate

Page 49

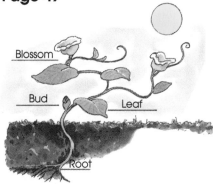

Blossom

Bud · Leaf

Root

Page 50

6, 2, 4
3, 1, 5

Page 51

1. soil
2. shoot
3. root
4. energy
5. buds
6. stem

E	N	E	R	G	Y	R	B	A
H	L	F	S	O	I	L	H	X
D	K	W	T	X	B	Z	R	B
F	N	S	D	C	N	F	O	R
O	S	T	C	B	T	P	O	H
I	T	Z	M	U	R	V	T	Y
V	E	T	R	D	V	S	N	E
K	M	W	F	S	H	O	O	T
U	P	O	T	B	I	H	L	P

Page 53

1. carbon dioxide
2. from animals
3. oxygen
4. from plants

Page 54

1. tomato
2. bean
3. corn
4. lily

Page 55

1. plant C
2. 3"
3. plants A and D

Page 57

1. food
2. seeds
3. hide
4. bury
5. carry
6. drop

Page 58

1. root
2. kernels or seeds
3. leaf

Pages 59–60

Children should list fruits and vegetables, other articles of clothing, one product such as maple syrup that comes from trees, and one plant-eating animal, such as sheep.

Page 61

1. true
2. false
3. false
4. false
5. true
6. false
7. true
8. true
9. false
10. true

More About Seeds and Plants

Activity Books
Exploring the World of Plants by Penny Raife Durant
The Science Book of Things That Grow by Neil Ardley
Science Crafts for Kids by Gwen Diehn and Terry Krautwurst

Information Books
Flowers, Fruits, Seeds by Jerome Wexler
From Seed to Plant by Gail Gibbons
The Hidden Magic of Seeds by Dorothy E. Shuttlesworth
How a Seed Grows by Helene J. Jordan
How Do Apples Grow? by Betsy Maestro
How Seeds Travel by Cynthia Overbeck
The Magic School Bus Plants Seeds by Patricia Rief

Storybooks
Anna in the Garden by Diane Dawson Hearn
The Green Man by Gail E. Haley
The Pea Patch Jig by Thatcher Hurd
Sunflower House by Eve Bunting
A Weed Is a Seed by Ferida Wolff

Audiotapes
Evergreen, Everblue by Raffi
Let's Clean Up Our Act: Songs for the Earth
   by Tom Callinan and Ann Shapiro

Videos
Flowers, Plants and Trees by Prism Entertainment
Look What I Grew by Intervideo
The Magic School Bus Goes to Seed distributed by KidVision

CD-ROMs
Let's Explore the Jungle by Humongous Entertainment
Microsoft Explorapedia for Windows: The World of Nature
A World of Plants by National Geographic Society